Generative AI Business Applications

Contents

Part I: Introduction to Generative AI in Business..4

  Understanding Generative AI 4

    What is Generative AI? 4

    Key Concepts and Technologies 5

    History and Evolution of Generative AI..6

  Generative AI and Business Transformation..7

    The Impact of Generative AI on Industries 7

    Opportunities and Challenges 8

    Case Studies of Business Transformation 9

Part II: Core Technologies and Techniques 10

  Generative Models and Architectures 10

    Generative Adversarial Networks (GANs)..10

    Variational Autoencoders (VAEs) 11

    Transformers and Large Language Models (LLMs)...12

  Data Preparation and Management..13

    Data Collection and Cleaning...13

    Data Augmentation Techniques 14

    Managing and Storing Large Datasets...15

  Training Generative Models 16

    Setting Up Training Environments..16

    Model Training Workflows 17

    Hyperparameter Tuning 18

Part III: Business Applications of Generative AI..19

  Content Creation and Media 19

    Automated Content Generation..19

    Generative Art and Design...20

    AI in Film and Music Production 21

  Customer Engagement and Personalization...21

    Personalized Marketing Campaigns 21

    AI-Driven Customer Service and Support 22

    Chatbots and Virtual Assistants 23

  Product and Service Innovation..23

    AI-Enhanced Product Design 23

    Rapid Prototyping with AI...24

    Customization and Mass Personalization 24

  Operational Efficiency and Optimization 25

    Supply Chain and Logistics Optimization 25

    Predictive Maintenance and Operations 26

    AI in Financial Forecasting and Risk Management 26

    Chapter: Redefining Customer Engagement with Hyper-Personalization 27

    Chapter: Optimizing Business Operations with Generative AI 37

    Chapter: Transforming Product Design and Prototyping 41

Part IV: Implementing Generative AI in Business 50

  Integration with Existing Systems 50

    APIs and Middleware Solutions 50

    Cloud Platforms and Services 51

    Ensuring Compatibility and Interoperability 52

  Deploying Generative AI Solutions 53

    Deployment Strategies and Best Practices 53

    Monitoring and Maintaining AI Systems 54

    Scalability and Performance Optimization 55

  Ethical and Regulatory Considerations 57

    Addressing Bias and Fairness 57

    Ensuring Transparency and Accountability 58

    Navigating Legal and Regulatory Frameworks 59

Part V: Advanced Topics and Future Trends 60

  Innovative Use Cases and Emerging Trends 61

    AI in Healthcare and Life Sciences 61

    AI in Finance and Insurance 61

    AI in Retail and E-commerce 62

  Future of Generative AI in Business 63

    Predictions and Future Directions 64

    Preparing for the Next Wave of AI Innovation 64

    Long-Term Implications for Businesses 65

Part VI: Hands-On Projects and Case Studies 66

  Practical Projects with Generative AI 67

    Building a Text Generation Model for Marketing 67

    Creating a Generative Art Application for Branding 67

    Developing a Chatbot for Customer Service 68

  Case Studies in Business Applications 69

Generative AI in a Leading Retailer 70

AI-Driven Innovation in a Manufacturing Firm 70

Transforming Customer Experience in Financial Services 71

Part I: Introduction to Generative AI in Business

Understanding Generative AI

What is Generative AI?

Generative AI refers to a subset of artificial intelligence that focuses on creating new content or data that is similar to existing data. Unlike traditional AI models that recognize patterns or make predictions, generative AI models are capable of producing original outputs such as text, images, music, and even complex data structures. These models learn the underlying patterns and structures of the input data and generate new data that follows the same patterns.

Generative AI is powered by advanced machine learning algorithms, particularly those based on deep learning. These models have vast applications, from creating realistic images and videos to generating human-like text and simulating complex processes.

Key Concepts and Technologies

1. **Generative Adversarial Networks (GANs):** GANs consist of two neural networks, a generator and a discriminator, that are trained simultaneously. The generator creates new data instances, while the discriminator evaluates them. The goal is for the generator to produce data that is indistinguishable from real data, thereby "fooling" the discriminator.

2. **Variational Autoencoders (VAEs):** VAEs are a type of autoencoder that learns a latent space representation of the input data. They can generate new data by sampling from the latent space, making them useful for applications like image synthesis and data augmentation.

3. **Transformers and Large Language Models (LLMs):** Transformers are a type of neural network architecture designed for handling sequential data, making them ideal for natural language processing tasks. LLMs, such as GPT (Generative Pre-trained Transformer), use transformers to generate human-like text based on the input data they are trained on.

History and Evolution of Generative AI

The concept of generative AI has evolved significantly over the past few decades. Early AI systems focused on rule-based approaches and simple statistical methods. The advent of deep learning in the early 2010s marked a significant shift, enabling the development of more sophisticated generative models. The introduction of GANs by Ian Goodfellow in 2014 was a major breakthrough, leading to rapid advancements in generative capabilities. Since then, the field has seen the emergence of powerful models like VAEs and transformers, which have pushed the boundaries of what generative AI can achieve.

Generative AI and Business Transformation

The Impact of Generative AI on Industries

Generative AI is transforming a wide range of industries by enabling new ways of creating content, optimizing processes, and enhancing customer experiences. For instance, in the media and entertainment industry, generative AI is used to create realistic visual effects, generate music, and automate content creation. In healthcare, it aids in drug discovery and the generation of synthetic medical data for research. In the retail sector, generative AI powers personalized marketing campaigns and product recommendations.

Opportunities and Challenges

Opportunities:

- **Innovation:** Generative AI enables businesses to innovate by creating new products and services that were previously impossible.

- **Efficiency:** Automating content creation and data generation can significantly reduce costs and increase efficiency.

- **Personalization:** Generative AI allows for highly personalized customer experiences, leading to increased customer satisfaction and loyalty.

Challenges:

- **Quality Control:** Ensuring the quality and reliability of generative outputs can be challenging.

- **Ethical Concerns:** The potential for misuse of generative AI, such as creating deepfakes, raises ethical and legal issues.

- **Technical Complexity:** Implementing and maintaining generative AI systems requires significant technical expertise and resources.

Case Studies of Business Transformation

1. **Media and Entertainment:** A major film studio uses GANs to create realistic visual effects, reducing the time and cost of post-production. This has enabled the studio to produce high-quality films faster and more economically.

2. **Healthcare:** A pharmaceutical company leverages VAEs to generate synthetic medical data, accelerating drug discovery and reducing the reliance on costly clinical trials. This approach has led to the development of new treatments and therapies.

3. **Retail:** An e-commerce platform utilizes transformers to generate personalized product descriptions and recommendations, enhancing the shopping experience and increasing sales conversion rates.

Part II: Core Technologies and Techniques

Generative Models and Architectures

Generative Adversarial Networks (GANs)

GANs are a class of machine learning frameworks where two neural networks contest with each other in a game. One network generates candidates (the generator) and the other evaluates them (the discriminator). This process continues until the generator produces outputs that are indistinguishable from the real data.

- **Generator:** Creates fake data from random noise.
- **Discriminator:** Distinguishes between real and fake data.

The training process involves the generator improving its ability to create realistic data, while the discriminator gets better at identifying fake data. This adversarial process pushes both networks to improve, resulting in high-quality generated data.

Variational Autoencoders (VAEs)

VAEs are a type of generative model that learn to encode input data into a latent space and then decode from this space to reconstruct the input data. The key innovation of VAEs is their ability to learn a smooth and continuous latent space, from which new data samples can be generated by sampling and decoding.

- **Encoder:** Compresses the input data into a latent space representation.
- **Decoder:** Reconstructs the input data from the latent space representation.

VAEs are particularly useful for tasks such as image synthesis, data compression, and anomaly detection.

Transformers and Large Language Models (LLMs)

Transformers are a type of neural network architecture designed to handle sequential data, making them particularly effective for natural language processing tasks. They use self-attention mechanisms to weigh the importance of different words in a sentence, allowing them to capture long-range dependencies in text.

- **Self-Attention Mechanism:** Enables the model to focus on different parts of the input sequence.
- **Positional Encoding:** Provides information about the position of words in the sequence.

LLMs, such as GPT-3, are built on transformer architectures and are pre-trained on vast amounts of text data. These models can generate coherent and contextually relevant text, making them valuable for applications like chatbots, content creation, and language translation.

Data Preparation and Management

Data Collection and Cleaning

The success of generative AI models depends on the quality of the data they are trained on. Data collection involves gathering relevant data from various sources, while data cleaning ensures that the data is accurate, consistent, and free of errors.

- **Data Collection:** Involves sourcing data from databases, APIs, web scraping, and other methods.
- **Data Cleaning:** Includes tasks such as removing duplicates, handling missing values, and correcting errors.

Effective data collection and cleaning are crucial for building robust generative models that produce high-quality outputs.

Data Augmentation Techniques

Data augmentation involves generating additional training data by applying transformations to the existing data. This technique is especially useful in scenarios where limited data is available.

- **Image Augmentation:** Techniques such as rotation, flipping, and scaling are used to generate more diverse training images.

- **Text Augmentation:** Methods like synonym replacement, random insertion, and back-translation are applied to create varied text samples.

Data augmentation helps improve the generalization ability of generative models by exposing them to a wider range of data variations.

Managing and Storing Large Datasets

Managing and storing large datasets requires efficient data management strategies and storage solutions. This involves using scalable storage systems, data indexing, and efficient retrieval methods.

- **Scalable Storage Systems:** Cloud storage solutions like AWS S3, Google Cloud Storage, and Azure Blob Storage provide scalable and reliable storage for large datasets.

- **Data Indexing:** Techniques such as database indexing and data partitioning enable fast and efficient data retrieval.

Effective data management ensures that the data is readily accessible and can be used efficiently during the training of generative models.

Training Generative Models

Setting Up Training Environments

Setting up an appropriate training environment is crucial for training generative models. This involves selecting the right hardware, software, and frameworks.

- **Hardware:** High-performance GPUs or TPUs are typically used to accelerate the training process.

- **Software and Frameworks:** Popular frameworks like TensorFlow, PyTorch, and Keras provide tools and libraries for building and training generative models.

A well-configured training environment ensures efficient and effective model training.

Model Training Workflows

The model training workflow involves several stages, including data preparation, model initialization, training, and evaluation.

1. **Data Preparation:** Preprocess the data and split it into training, validation, and test sets.

2. **Model Initialization:** Define the model architecture and initialize the parameters.

3. **Training:** Train the model using the training data, optimizing the loss function.

4. **Evaluation:** Evaluate the model performance using validation and test data.

Following a structured training workflow ensures that the generative model is trained effectively and can generalize well to new data.

Hyperparameter Tuning

Hyperparameter tuning involves adjusting the hyperparameters of the generative model to optimize its performance. This process can be time-consuming but is essential for achieving the best results.

- **Grid Search:** A systematic approach to try different combinations of hyperparameters.

- **Random Search:** Randomly samples hyperparameter combinations to explore a wider range of possibilities.

- **Bayesian Optimization:** Uses probabilistic models to find the optimal hyperparameters efficiently.

Effective hyperparameter tuning can significantly improve the performance of generative models, leading to higher quality and more reliable outputs.

Part III: Business Applications of Generative AI

Content Creation and Media

Automated Content Generation

Generative AI can automate the creation of various types of content, significantly reducing the time and effort required to produce high-quality materials. This includes writing articles, generating social media posts, creating marketing copy, and more. By analyzing large datasets of existing content, generative AI models can understand language patterns and generate coherent and contextually relevant text. This technology is particularly useful for content-heavy industries like publishing, advertising, and digital marketing.

Generative Art and Design

In the realm of art and design, generative AI offers innovative ways to create original artwork, design elements, and digital assets. Artists and designers can use AI tools to explore new creative possibilities, from generating unique patterns and textures to designing entire pieces of digital art. This technology democratizes creativity, allowing individuals with limited artistic skills to produce professional-quality work. Generative AI can also assist in designing logos, branding materials, and product packaging, enhancing the creative process and expanding artistic horizons.

AI in Film and Music Production

The film and music industries are harnessing the power of generative AI to streamline production processes and enhance creative output. In film production, AI can generate realistic special effects, create synthetic actors, and even write scripts. This reduces production costs and accelerates timelines. In music production, AI can compose original music, generate accompaniment tracks, and assist in mixing and mastering. By analyzing existing music, generative AI models can create new compositions that mimic specific styles or genres, offering a valuable tool for musicians and producers.

Customer Engagement and Personalization

Personalized Marketing Campaigns

Generative AI enables highly personalized marketing campaigns by analyzing customer data and generating tailored content. This includes personalized emails, targeted advertisements, and customized product recommendations. By understanding individual preferences and behaviors, generative AI can create marketing messages that resonate with customers, increasing engagement and conversion rates. This level of personalization enhances the customer experience and strengthens brand loyalty.

AI-Driven Customer Service and Support

Customer service and support can be significantly enhanced with AI-driven solutions. Generative AI can automate responses to customer inquiries, providing instant support and freeing up human agents to handle more complex issues. AI-driven chatbots and virtual assistants can understand and respond to a wide range of customer queries, improving response times and customer satisfaction. Additionally, generative AI can analyze customer interactions to identify common issues and suggest improvements to service processes.

Chatbots and Virtual Assistants

Chatbots and virtual assistants powered by generative AI are becoming increasingly sophisticated and capable of handling a variety of tasks. These AI-driven tools can assist customers with information retrieval, product recommendations, and transaction processing. They can engage in natural, human-like conversations, providing a seamless and efficient customer experience. Businesses are leveraging these tools to enhance customer support, reduce operational costs, and provide 24/7 assistance.

Product and Service Innovation

AI-Enhanced Product Design

Generative AI is revolutionizing product design by enabling rapid prototyping and iterative design processes. AI can generate multiple design options based on predefined parameters, allowing designers to explore a wide range of possibilities quickly. This technology can optimize designs for functionality, aesthetics, and manufacturability, leading to innovative and efficient products. Industries such as automotive, consumer electronics, and fashion are leveraging generative AI to push the boundaries of product design and development.

Rapid Prototyping with AI

Rapid prototyping with AI accelerates the development of new products by automating the creation of prototypes. Generative AI can produce detailed 3D models and simulations, allowing designers to test and refine their ideas quickly. This reduces the time and cost associated with traditional prototyping methods. AI-driven rapid prototyping is particularly valuable in industries where speed to market is critical, such as technology and consumer goods.

Customization and Mass Personalization

Generative AI enables businesses to offer customized and personalized products at scale. By analyzing customer preferences and behaviors, AI can generate bespoke designs and configurations tailored to individual needs. This approach is transforming industries like fashion, where personalized clothing and accessories can be created on-demand, and consumer electronics, where custom configurations can be offered. Mass personalization enhances customer satisfaction and provides a competitive edge in crowded markets.

Operational Efficiency and Optimization

Supply Chain and Logistics Optimization

Generative AI is optimizing supply chain and logistics operations by analyzing vast amounts of data and generating efficient solutions. AI can predict demand, optimize inventory levels, and streamline transportation routes. This reduces costs, minimizes waste, and improves overall supply chain efficiency. Businesses in retail, manufacturing, and logistics are leveraging generative AI to enhance their supply chain operations and improve responsiveness to market changes.

Predictive Maintenance and Operations

Predictive maintenance powered by generative AI helps businesses avoid costly downtime and extend the lifespan of their equipment. By analyzing data from sensors and historical maintenance records, AI models can predict when equipment is likely to fail and recommend proactive maintenance. This approach reduces unplanned downtime, lowers maintenance costs, and improves operational efficiency. Industries such as manufacturing, energy, and transportation are using generative AI to implement predictive maintenance strategies and optimize their operations.

AI in Financial Forecasting and Risk Management

In the financial sector, generative AI is enhancing forecasting and risk management capabilities. AI models can analyze historical data and market trends to generate accurate financial forecasts, helping businesses make informed decisions. Additionally, generative AI can identify and assess potential risks, providing insights that enable proactive risk management. Financial institutions, investment firms, and businesses across various industries are leveraging generative AI to improve their financial planning and

risk mitigation strategies.

Chapter: Redefining Customer Engagement with Hyper-Personalization

Generative AI is at the forefront of a profound transformation in customer engagement, enabling businesses to deliver hyper-personalized experiences that were once unachievable. Through predictive modeling, advanced natural language generation, and real-time data processing, generative AI is allowing companies to understand, anticipate, and cater to customer needs in ways that drive loyalty and enhance satisfaction. In this chapter, we explore how companies across industries are leveraging generative AI to redefine customer engagement strategies, from personalized content delivery to real-time customer support and beyond.

At the core of generative AI's impact on customer engagement is its ability to drive hyper-personalization at scale. Traditional personalization efforts were often limited by segmented audience data, delivering recommendations based on broad demographic information or past behaviors. Generative AI, however, enables a granular understanding of individual customer preferences, creating highly tailored experiences. For instance, e-commerce platforms like Amazon use generative AI models to recommend products not only based on purchase history but also considering contextual data, such as time of day, location, and even the latest trends on social media. This real-time personalization allows companies to anticipate customer needs more accurately and present products or services that feel uniquely suited to each individual.

In the media and entertainment industry, companies are using generative AI to create personalized content recommendations and even generate original content. Netflix, for instance, relies on generative AI to analyze user behavior patterns and recommend shows or movies that align with each subscriber's preferences. Beyond recommending existing content, Netflix is now exploring AI-driven content generation to develop trailers, promotional visuals, and potentially even custom plot variations tailored to different audience segments. This move represents a paradigm shift where content is not only consumed in a personalized way but created to match user interests, making engagement deeper and more immersive.

Generative AI's capabilities extend to the advertising industry, where it enables brands to produce personalized marketing campaigns at unprecedented scale. Dynamic ad content generation allows brands to create multiple variations of an ad, each tailored to specific audience segments. For instance, a travel company can use generative AI to create ads showing different destinations based on the browsing history of the viewer. A customer browsing beach destinations may see ads promoting tropical vacations, while another interested in adventure travel might see promotions for mountain resorts. This targeted approach enhances click-through rates and conversion rates, as customers are more likely to engage with ads that resonate with their preferences.

Generative AI is also transforming how businesses manage customer communication. Chatbots and virtual assistants, powered by advanced large language models, now offer near-human conversational capabilities, enabling real-time customer support and engagement. Unlike traditional scripted chatbots, generative AI-driven assistants can handle complex queries, adapt to the conversational tone of the customer, and even detect sentiment to adjust their responses. Companies like Bank of America and Sephora have integrated AI-driven chatbots into their customer service operations, allowing them to provide 24/7 support with high levels of customer satisfaction. These bots are capable of handling a wide range of customer interactions, from answering frequently asked questions to assisting with purchases, thereby freeing up human agents to focus on more complex issues.

In the retail sector, generative AI-driven virtual try-on features are becoming increasingly popular. Using AI-powered image generation, companies can allow customers to visualize how products—such as clothing, makeup, or eyewear—will look on them before making a purchase. For example, Sephora's AI-powered makeup try-on tool lets customers see how different products will look on their skin tones by uploading a selfie. This interactive experience enhances customer engagement and helps build confidence in purchasing decisions, thereby reducing return rates and improving customer satisfaction. Retailers are investing heavily in these virtual experiences, as they not only attract a larger customer base but also provide valuable data that can inform future product recommendations.

Generative AI's ability to create unique customer profiles is particularly valuable in the finance industry, where institutions can use AI-driven insights to recommend products that align with each client's financial goals. Traditional customer segmentation in finance often relies on broad demographic information, but generative AI allows for far more sophisticated segmentation by examining behavioral patterns, spending habits, and personal milestones. For instance, a bank might use AI to predict when a customer is likely to consider buying a home based on their spending and saving patterns, and proactively offer mortgage options or financial planning services.

This level of personalization builds trust and encourages clients to deepen their relationship with the financial institution.

In addition to providing targeted product recommendations, generative AI is improving customer engagement by personalizing educational content. Banks and financial services can offer generative AI-powered tutorials, articles, or video content that explain complex financial concepts tailored to each customer's knowledge level and financial goals. A novice investor might receive simple articles on budgeting and saving, while a more experienced investor could be offered insights into portfolio diversification and risk management. This tailored educational approach helps clients feel more informed and supported, building a positive relationship with the brand.

Generative AI's role in optimizing customer engagement extends to real-time sentiment analysis. By analyzing customer interactions across touchpoints, generative AI can identify and respond to emotions, allowing companies to proactively address dissatisfaction or enhance positive experiences. For instance, during a customer service interaction, AI can detect if a customer is frustrated and trigger a more empathetic response or even escalate the case to a human representative. This capability enables businesses to resolve issues quickly and effectively, turning potentially negative interactions into positive outcomes.

Moreover, real-time sentiment analysis is allowing companies to better understand brand perception and customer loyalty. AI tools can process social media posts, reviews, and other user-generated content to gauge public sentiment about a brand or product. By continuously monitoring this feedback, companies can make informed decisions about product changes, marketing strategies, or customer engagement initiatives. For example, a restaurant chain may use sentiment analysis to understand how new menu items are being received, adjusting recipes or promotional strategies accordingly. This real-time feedback loop enables businesses to stay agile and responsive to customer needs, ultimately enhancing satisfaction and loyalty.

Generative AI is also enhancing loyalty programs, making them more dynamic and rewarding. Rather than offering generic points-based rewards, companies can use AI to create personalized loyalty offers that align with individual shopping habits and preferences. For instance, a retailer could offer a unique discount on a product category that the customer frequently purchases, or a hotel chain could tailor loyalty perks to match the traveler's preferences, such as room upgrades or dining credits. These tailored rewards make loyalty programs more meaningful to customers, driving engagement and repeat business. Businesses across sectors are increasingly recognizing the power of personalized loyalty programs and investing in AI to make these programs more relevant to each customer.

Another area where generative AI is making an impact is in customer feedback collection and analysis. Traditional surveys often suffer from low response rates and limited insights. Generative AI, however, can analyze customer conversations, reviews, and support tickets to derive meaningful insights without requiring explicit feedback. For instance, an AI system can analyze call center transcripts to identify common issues, recurring product complaints, or service gaps. This approach allows businesses to gain deeper insights into customer sentiment and preferences, helping them improve their products and services without relying on traditional feedback mechanisms.

Finally, generative AI is enhancing customer experience through personalized recommendations that evolve over time. Unlike traditional recommendation engines that primarily rely on past behavior, generative AI considers changes in customer preferences, market trends, and contextual factors. For example, streaming platforms like Spotify and Apple Music use generative AI to create personalized playlists that adapt to each user's evolving tastes. These adaptive recommendations keep users engaged by providing fresh content that aligns with their current mood or interests, thereby increasing user satisfaction and retention.

In conclusion, generative AI is reshaping customer engagement by delivering highly personalized, real-time experiences across industries. From dynamic ad content to hyper-personalized recommendations and AI-driven sentiment analysis, businesses are using generative AI to connect with customers on a deeper level. As generative AI technology continues to advance, companies that embrace these tools for customer engagement will gain a competitive edge, driving loyalty and enhancing customer satisfaction.

Chapter: Optimizing Business Operations with Generative AI

Generative AI's potential extends far beyond customer-facing applications, playing a transformative role in internal business operations. Organizations increasingly leverage AI-driven automation, predictive analytics, and optimization tools to enhance productivity, streamline workflows, and make informed strategic decisions. By automating routine tasks, improving supply chain efficiency, and supporting data-driven insights, generative AI is redefining operational excellence across industries. In this chapter, we delve into the advanced applications of generative AI in optimizing business operations, highlighting real-world examples, benefits, and challenges.

A primary advantage of generative AI in business operations is its ability to automate complex tasks that require extensive data processing, logical decision-making, or predictive analysis. Traditional automation has been useful for streamlining straightforward, rule-based tasks; however, generative AI pushes these boundaries, enabling more sophisticated automation that adapts to context and changing conditions. For instance, AI-driven automation in finance can handle intricate tasks such as fraud detection, risk assessment, and regulatory compliance. Banks and financial institutions utilize generative AI to monitor and analyze vast quantities of transaction data in real-time, identifying patterns and flagging unusual behavior that may indicate fraudulent activity. This proactive approach helps prevent fraud and reduces financial loss.

In manufacturing, generative AI is revolutionizing supply chain management and production processes. Advanced AI models can predict demand with remarkable accuracy, allowing companies to adjust their production schedules and inventory levels accordingly. By processing data from sources such as historical sales, weather forecasts, and economic indicators, generative AI predicts demand spikes or drops, helping manufacturers optimize their production and reduce waste. For example, Toyota leverages AI-driven predictive maintenance to forecast when machinery will need servicing, minimizing downtime and ensuring continuous production flow. This predictive approach allows manufacturers to avoid costly interruptions and extend the lifespan of their equipment, resulting in significant cost savings.

Generative AI's role in optimizing supply chains also extends to logistics and distribution. Companies can use AI models to simulate various supply chain scenarios, allowing them to prepare for disruptions such as supplier delays, transportation bottlenecks, or geopolitical factors. For example, logistics companies like DHL and UPS employ generative AI to optimize route planning, dynamically adjusting routes based on real-time traffic and weather data. This agility reduces fuel costs, enhances delivery speed, and improves customer satisfaction. In addition, AI-driven insights into warehouse management are helping companies streamline inventory storage, optimize picking routes, and reduce operational costs. Generative AI allows businesses to maintain leaner inventories while ensuring they can meet demand, resulting in greater operational efficiency and cost-effectiveness.

Generative AI is also transforming business operations by enhancing strategic decision-making through predictive analytics. Advanced AI models can analyze vast datasets and generate insights that inform critical business decisions, from market expansion to product development. By processing historical data, customer feedback, and market trends, generative AI identifies patterns and correlations that may not be apparent to human analysts. For example, retailers like Walmart use generative AI to forecast market demand and adjust inventory and pricing strategies accordingly. This proactive approach enables retailers to stay competitive and meet customer needs without overstocking or understocking products.

In the financial sector, generative AI is a powerful tool for investment firms, providing portfolio optimization and risk management. AI models analyze historical price data

Chapter: Transforming Product Design and Prototyping

Generative AI is revolutionizing the product design process by allowing businesses to quickly iterate on concepts, test feasibility, and reduce time-to-market. Traditionally, the design and prototyping process could take months, requiring intensive collaboration between designers, engineers, and often feedback from early focus groups. With generative AI, product teams can rapidly develop, test, and refine designs, harnessing data-driven insights to produce more effective and customer-centric products.

Generative AI-driven design tools have emerged as crucial allies in this transformation, offering businesses an unprecedented ability to blend design intuition with data-driven iterations. For instance, tools like Autodesk's Dreamcatcher or generative design software that employs GANs (Generative Adversarial Networks) can automatically produce thousands of potential design configurations based on input parameters, such as material strength, cost, or weight. The system evaluates each design variation and highlights optimal configurations, which are then refined further by human designers.

These tools don't just make the design process faster; they improve the quality and functionality of the final product by exploring configurations beyond what human designers might initially conceive. For example, an automobile company might use generative AI to design car parts that are both lighter and more robust, optimizing fuel efficiency and vehicle performance.

For fashion and apparel industries, generative AI offers even greater flexibility, enabling brands to keep up with fast-changing consumer tastes. By using customer data, such as past purchase history, seasonality preferences, and social media behavior, generative AI algorithms can create designs that align with current trends. Companies like Zalando and Stitch Fix are already leveraging this capability, utilizing AI to suggest product lines tailored to unique customer segments. The output is not merely a product recommendation but an entirely new line of products informed by generative insights.

Generative AI is also enabling hyper-personalization in products. This trend is particularly valuable in the luxury goods sector, where customization is a key value proposition. By analyzing customer data, brands can create one-of-a-kind items that reflect individual customer preferences. For instance, high-end car manufacturers can offer custom-designed interior elements that match each buyer's aesthetic preferences, from the shape and color of the seats to the textures and finishes on the dashboard. AI-powered platforms analyze customer tastes and auto-generate possible designs for clients to choose from, cutting the time needed for custom design and production.

Another powerful use of generative AI in product development is rapid prototyping. In the traditional model, prototyping could be costly and time-consuming, often requiring multiple iterations and testing. Generative AI shortens this cycle by creating virtual prototypes that are tested in simulation environments. For instance, Boeing uses generative design to create lightweight and strong aircraft parts, which are then tested for aerodynamic efficiency and structural integrity within a virtual model of an aircraft. This approach significantly reduces the cost of physical prototyping and allows Boeing to simulate extreme conditions, such as wind speeds and stress, without needing a physical model.

Generative AI's impact on manufacturing is significant as well. Companies can optimize design configurations for efficient manufacturing, reducing both waste and production costs. By training generative algorithms on past production data, manufacturers can identify designs that minimize material use while maintaining quality. For instance, Adidas uses generative AI to improve the performance of its footwear by adjusting design parameters to achieve both comfort and durability. With each iteration, generative AI systems learn from production data to refine future designs, reducing waste and creating a more sustainable manufacturing process.

Beyond industrial applications, generative AI is making waves in digital products and services. For instance, video game developers leverage generative AI to create immersive environments, characters, and narratives. By analyzing player preferences and in-game behavior, generative AI can develop unique story arcs and world elements, making each user's experience distinct. Platforms like Unity are increasingly embedding AI tools that allow developers to customize game mechanics, characters, and settings on-the-fly, based on user inputs. This creates games that feel more responsive and personalized, enhancing user engagement and extending game lifespan.

Moreover, the integration of generative AI into augmented reality (AR) and virtual reality (VR) systems promises even greater advancements in product design. For instance, home interior brands use generative AI to help customers visualize customized interior designs in VR. Customers can adjust parameters like room layout, furniture style, and color scheme, and the AI system generates 3D visualizations in real-time. This interactivity empowers customers to take a more active role in design while helping businesses meet customer needs more precisely. Home improvement companies are increasingly investing in these types of applications, as they see a growing market for self-service design solutions that allow customers to "see" their vision come to life before any construction begins.

The automotive industry is also exploring generative AI for designing vehicle interfaces, like dashboards and infotainment systems. Using AI-generated insights on user preferences and ergonomics, companies can produce interfaces that prioritize usability and aesthetic appeal. By leveraging large amounts of customer data, companies like Tesla and BMW design dashboards that feel intuitive and engaging. The AI considers how users interact with similar interfaces, refining its suggestions to produce better, user-friendly layouts. This capability not only improves user satisfaction but also shortens the design cycle, as fewer user testing cycles are needed to achieve a successful interface.

Another example is found in consumer electronics, where generative AI aids in designing devices that are highly functional yet compact. AI-driven design algorithms analyze ergonomic data and user feedback to create devices with optimized layouts. For example, smartphone manufacturers use generative AI to design motherboards and internal components, arranging them to minimize space without compromising performance. By harnessing AI, companies can also create modular and customizable devices, catering to specific user preferences in terms of features and design. This approach is becoming more common among manufacturers as consumers demand more tailored experiences and businesses seek new ways to differentiate themselves in a crowded market.

Looking forward, businesses are beginning to explore generative AI's potential in designing eco-friendly products. Companies are training AI algorithms on sustainability metrics, such as energy use, carbon footprint, and recyclability, to create designs that are not only innovative but also sustainable. For example, furniture companies are exploring generative AI to design products that use less material without sacrificing durability. These designs minimize waste and reduce the environmental impact of production, aligning with growing consumer demand for sustainable products. In architecture, firms use generative AI to develop energy-efficient building designs, optimizing structures for natural lighting and ventilation to reduce energy consumption.

Generative AI's role in product design and prototyping is set to expand as businesses integrate it further into their workflows. With continued advancements in computing power and AI algorithms, companies can expect even faster, more efficient design cycles that yield high-quality, innovative products. For businesses, this shift means adopting an iterative, data-driven design approach that prioritizes both customer satisfaction and operational efficiency.

As generative AI continues to mature, businesses that harness its capabilities for product design and prototyping will enjoy a significant competitive advantage. By improving their capacity to rapidly innovate and meet customer needs, they can better respond to market demands and stay ahead in an increasingly dynamic landscape. The next chapter will explore how generative AI is transforming customer engagement, enabling highly personalized experiences and reshaping the way businesses interact with consumers in both digital and physical spaces.

Part IV: Implementing Generative AI in Business

Integration with Existing Systems

APIs and Middleware Solutions

Integrating generative AI into existing systems often requires the use of APIs (Application Programming Interfaces) and middleware solutions. APIs provide a standardized way for different software applications to communicate and exchange data. They enable businesses to incorporate AI functionalities without needing to rebuild their entire infrastructure.

Middleware solutions act as intermediaries that manage the interaction between different systems. They ensure seamless integration by handling data translation, message routing, and other interoperability tasks. By leveraging APIs and middleware, businesses can integrate generative AI models with their current systems, ensuring a smooth transition and minimal disruption.

Cloud Platforms and Services

Cloud platforms and services offer scalable and flexible solutions for deploying generative AI models. Major cloud providers like Amazon Web Services (AWS), Google Cloud Platform (GCP), and Microsoft Azure offer a range of AI and machine learning services that simplify the deployment process. These platforms provide the necessary computational power, storage, and tools to develop, train, and deploy AI models efficiently.

Cloud services also offer pre-built AI models, data management tools, and integration capabilities, reducing the time and resources required to implement generative AI. By using cloud platforms, businesses can scale their AI solutions as needed, ensuring they meet the demands of their operations.

Ensuring Compatibility and Interoperability

Ensuring compatibility and interoperability between generative AI models and existing systems is crucial for successful implementation. This involves:

- **Data Compatibility:** Ensuring that the data formats used by AI models are compatible with existing data sources and systems.

- **System Interoperability:** Ensuring that AI models can interact seamlessly with other software applications and platforms.

- **Standardization:** Using industry-standard protocols and formats to facilitate integration and communication between systems.

Compatibility and interoperability ensure that generative AI solutions can be effectively integrated into the business workflow, providing the desired benefits without causing disruptions.

Deploying Generative AI Solutions

Deployment Strategies and Best Practices

Deploying generative AI solutions involves several strategic considerations to ensure successful implementation. Key strategies and best practices include:

- **Incremental Deployment:** Start with pilot projects to test and refine the AI models before full-scale deployment. This allows for adjustments based on initial feedback and performance.

- **Cross-Functional Collaboration:** Involve stakeholders from different departments (e.g., IT, operations, marketing) to ensure the AI solution meets the needs of various business functions.

- **Clear Objectives:** Define clear objectives and success metrics for the AI deployment to measure its impact and effectiveness.

- **Continuous Improvement:** Continuously monitor and improve the AI models based on performance data and user feedback.

Following these strategies helps ensure that the deployment of generative AI solutions is aligned with business goals and delivers tangible benefits.

Monitoring and Maintaining AI Systems

Once generative AI solutions are deployed, continuous monitoring and maintenance are essential to ensure they function effectively and deliver consistent results. Key aspects include:

- **Performance Monitoring:** Regularly track the performance of AI models to identify any issues or deviations from expected behavior.

- **Error Handling:** Implement mechanisms to detect and address errors or anomalies in the AI outputs.

- **Model Updates:** Periodically update the AI models with new data and retrain them to maintain accuracy and relevance.

- **Security:** Ensure that AI systems are secure from potential threats and vulnerabilities.

Effective monitoring and maintenance help sustain the performance of generative AI solutions and adapt to changing business needs.

Scalability and Performance Optimization

Scalability and performance optimization are critical for ensuring that generative AI solutions can handle increasing workloads and deliver fast, reliable results. Strategies for achieving scalability and performance optimization include:

- **Distributed Computing:** Use distributed computing frameworks to parallelize the training and inference processes, allowing the AI models to scale across multiple machines.
- **Hardware Acceleration:** Leverage specialized hardware, such as GPUs and TPUs, to accelerate the computational tasks involved in training and running AI models.

- **Load Balancing:** Implement load balancing techniques to distribute workloads evenly across resources, preventing bottlenecks and ensuring smooth operation.

- **Resource Management:** Monitor and manage computational resources to ensure optimal utilization and cost efficiency.

By focusing on scalability and performance optimization, businesses can ensure that their generative AI solutions can grow with their needs and deliver consistent, high-quality results.

Ethical and Regulatory Considerations

Addressing Bias and Fairness

Generative AI models can inadvertently learn and propagate biases present in the training data. Addressing bias and ensuring fairness is crucial to building ethical AI systems. Strategies include:

- **Bias Detection:** Implement tools and techniques to detect and measure biases in AI models and outputs.

- **Diverse Data:** Use diverse and representative datasets to train AI models, reducing the risk of biased outcomes.

- **Fairness Algorithms:** Incorporate fairness algorithms that adjust the AI models to ensure equitable treatment of different groups.

- **Transparency:** Make the processes and decisions of AI systems transparent to users and stakeholders, enabling scrutiny and accountability.

Addressing bias and fairness ensures that generative AI solutions are ethical and do not perpetuate harmful stereotypes or discrimination.

Ensuring Transparency and Accountability

Transparency and accountability are essential for building trust in generative AI systems. This involves:

- **Explainable AI:** Develop AI models that provide explanations for their decisions and outputs, making it easier for users to understand how the AI works.
- **Documentation:** Maintain thorough documentation of AI models, including their development, training data, and performance metrics.

- **Stakeholder Engagement:** Involve stakeholders in the development and deployment process to ensure their concerns and expectations are addressed.

- **Audit Trails:** Implement audit trails to track the use and impact of AI systems, ensuring accountability for their actions and decisions.

Ensuring transparency and accountability helps build trust and confidence in generative AI solutions among users and stakeholders.

Navigating Legal and Regulatory Frameworks

As the use of generative AI grows, so does the need to navigate legal and regulatory frameworks. This involves:

- **Compliance:** Ensure that AI solutions comply with relevant laws and regulations, such as data protection and privacy laws.

- **Ethical Guidelines:** Adhere to ethical guidelines and industry standards for AI development and deployment.

- **Risk Management:** Identify and mitigate potential legal and regulatory risks associated with the use of generative AI.

- **Continuous Monitoring:** Stay updated with evolving legal and regulatory requirements to ensure ongoing compliance.

Part V: Advanced Topics and Future Trends

Innovative Use Cases and Emerging Trends

AI in Healthcare and Life Sciences

Generative AI is revolutionizing healthcare and life sciences by enabling breakthroughs in medical research, diagnostics, and personalized medicine. Key applications include:

- **Drug Discovery:** AI models generate new molecular structures, accelerating the identification of potential drug candidates and reducing the time and cost of drug development.

- **Medical Imaging:** AI enhances the analysis of medical images, assisting radiologists in detecting anomalies and diagnosing conditions more accurately and quickly.

- **Personalized Treatment:** AI-driven models analyze patient data to create personalized treatment plans, improving patient outcomes and optimizing healthcare resources.

AI in Finance and Insurance

In the finance and insurance sectors, generative AI is driving innovation and improving operational efficiency. Notable use cases include:

- **Fraud Detection:** AI models detect fraudulent activities by analyzing transaction patterns and identifying anomalies, enhancing security and reducing financial losses.

- **Risk Management:** AI assists in assessing and managing risks by analyzing large datasets and generating insights for better decision-making.

- **Customer Service:** AI-powered chatbots and virtual assistants provide personalized customer support, streamlining interactions and improving customer satisfaction.

AI in Retail and E-commerce

Generative AI is transforming the retail and e-commerce industries by enhancing customer experiences and optimizing operations. Key applications include:

- **Personalized Recommendations:** AI models generate personalized product recommendations based on customer preferences and browsing behavior, boosting sales and customer engagement.

- **Inventory Management:** AI predicts demand and optimizes inventory levels, reducing stockouts and overstock situations.

- **Virtual Try-Ons:** AI creates realistic virtual try-on experiences for fashion and beauty products, helping customers make informed purchasing decisions and reducing return rates.

Future of Generative AI in Business

Predictions and Future Directions

Generative AI is poised to become an integral part of business operations across various industries. Future directions include:

- **Enhanced Creativity:** AI will increasingly assist in creative processes, from content creation to product design, enabling businesses to innovate faster and more efficiently.

- **Human-AI Collaboration:** The synergy between human creativity and AI capabilities will drive new business models and opportunities, enhancing productivity and decision-making.

- **AI-Driven Automation:** More business processes will be automated using AI, leading to significant efficiency gains and cost reductions.

Preparing for the Next Wave of AI Innovation

Businesses must prepare for the next wave of AI innovation by:

- **Investing in AI Infrastructure:** Building robust AI infrastructure, including data management systems and computational resources, to support AI initiatives.

- **Upskilling Workforce:** Training employees in AI and machine learning skills to ensure they can effectively leverage AI tools and technologies.

- **Fostering Innovation:** Encouraging a culture of innovation and experimentation to identify new AI-driven opportunities and stay ahead of competitors.

Long-Term Implications for Businesses

The long-term implications of generative AI for businesses include:

- **Competitive Advantage:** Early adopters of generative AI will gain a significant competitive edge by leveraging AI to drive innovation and operational efficiency.

- **Business Model Transformation:** Generative AI will enable the creation of new business models and revenue streams, transforming industries and markets.

- **Ethical Considerations:** Businesses must address ethical considerations and ensure responsible AI use to build trust and maintain regulatory compliance.

Part VI: Hands-On Projects and Case Studies

Practical Projects with Generative AI

Building a Text Generation Model for Marketing

In this project, you will build a text generation model to create marketing copy. Steps include:

1. **Data Collection:** Gather a dataset of marketing texts, such as advertisements, social media posts, and email campaigns.

2. **Data Preprocessing:** Clean and preprocess the data to ensure it is suitable for training the AI model.

3. **Model Training:** Use a transformer-based model, such as GPT-3, to train the text generation model on the preprocessed data.

4. **Evaluation and Fine-Tuning:** Evaluate the model's performance and fine-tune it to improve the quality of the generated text.

5. **Deployment:** Deploy the model to generate marketing copy for various campaigns and measure its impact.

Creating a Generative Art Application for Branding

This project involves creating a generative art application to design unique branding materials. Steps include:

1. **Data Collection:** Collect a dataset of artwork and design elements that align with the brand's aesthetic.

2. **Model Training:** Train a generative adversarial network (GAN) on the dataset to generate new art and design elements.

3. **Application Development:** Develop a user-friendly application that allows users to generate and customize branding materials using the AI-generated designs.

4. **Evaluation:** Assess the quality and originality of the generated designs and iterate on the model as needed.

Developing a Chatbot for Customer Service

In this project, you will develop a chatbot to enhance customer service. Steps include:

1. **Data Collection:** Gather a dataset of customer service interactions, including common queries and responses.

2. **Model Training:** Train a conversational AI model, such as a transformer-based chatbot, on the dataset.

3. **Integration:** Integrate the chatbot with the existing customer service platform, ensuring it can handle various customer queries and provide accurate responses.

4. **Testing and Deployment:** Test the chatbot with real users, gather feedback, and refine its performance before full deployment.

Generative AI in a Leading Retailer

A leading retailer implemented generative AI to enhance its product recommendation system. By analyzing customer data and generating personalized recommendations, the retailer saw a significant increase in sales and customer engagement. The AI system also optimized inventory management, reducing costs and improving operational efficiency.

AI-Driven Innovation in a Manufacturing Firm

A manufacturing firm used generative AI to accelerate its product design and prototyping processes. The AI system generated multiple design options based on predefined parameters, allowing the firm to explore new designs quickly and cost-effectively. This led to the development of innovative products and a faster time-to-market.

Transforming Customer Experience in Financial Services

A financial services company leveraged generative AI to transform its customer experience. The company deployed AI-powered chatbots and virtual assistants to handle customer inquiries, providing instant support and personalized financial advice. This improved customer satisfaction and reduced operational costs. Additionally, AI-driven analytics helped the company identify and manage risks more effectively, enhancing its overall performance.

Chapter: Transforming Internal Operations with Generative AI

Generative AI's impact on business isn't limited to customer-facing applications; it is fundamentally transforming internal operations, enabling businesses to streamline processes, enhance supply chain management, and unlock predictive insights that drive competitive advantage. By automating routine tasks, generating actionable insights, and facilitating predictive analytics, generative AI is helping companies optimize their operations for greater efficiency, flexibility, and innovation.

Businesses are using generative AI to automate a wide range of repetitive tasks, freeing up human resources for more strategic and creative work. One of the most common applications is in document processing and data entry, where AI systems can extract, interpret, and organize data from invoices, purchase orders, contracts, and other documents. Companies like UiPath and Automation Anywhere provide AI-driven robotic process automation (RPA) platforms that streamline document-heavy workflows in industries such as finance, healthcare, and legal services. These AI-powered solutions can handle document classification, data extraction, and error detection at speeds and accuracies that human operators cannot match, significantly reducing processing times and error rates. By eliminating manual tasks, businesses not only cut costs but also enhance employee satisfaction by allowing teams to focus on more meaningful work.

Generative AI is also reshaping knowledge management within organizations. Traditionally, companies have struggled to harness the vast amount of information stored across databases, documents, and employee expertise. Generative AI-powered knowledge management systems are changing this by generating summaries, organizing content, and providing context-aware answers to employee queries. For example, companies can deploy AI-based assistants that allow employees to query internal documents, policies, and previous projects using natural language prompts. This enables employees to access information quickly and easily, reducing the time spent searching for information and improving productivity. Generative AI's ability to synthesize information from multiple sources makes it a valuable tool for knowledge management, facilitating better collaboration and decision-making across departments.

Supply chain management is another area where generative AI is having a transformative effect. From demand forecasting to logistics optimization, generative AI enables businesses to make data-driven decisions that improve supply chain resilience and efficiency. AI models can predict demand patterns by analyzing historical sales data, market trends, and external factors such as seasonality and economic indicators. These forecasts enable companies to adjust production schedules, manage inventory levels, and allocate resources more effectively, reducing the risk of stockouts and excess inventory. For instance, Coca-Cola uses AI to optimize its supply chain by predicting demand with high accuracy, enabling it to adjust its production and distribution processes in real-time. This level of agility is essential in today's fast-paced market environment, where unexpected changes in demand can have significant impacts on profitability.

Generative AI is also being used to optimize logistics within the supply chain, from route planning to warehouse management. AI algorithms analyze data from various sources, including GPS, traffic patterns, weather forecasts, and delivery schedules, to determine the most efficient routes for transportation. This not only reduces fuel costs but also improves delivery times, enhancing customer satisfaction. In warehouse management, generative AI can be used to optimize storage layouts, manage stock levels, and streamline picking and packing processes. For example, Amazon has implemented generative AI-powered robotics in its fulfillment centers to speed up order processing and reduce human labor requirements. These systems can autonomously navigate warehouses, pick items, and pack them, significantly increasing operational efficiency and reducing the risk of errors.

Moreover, generative AI is playing a crucial role in quality control within manufacturing processes. Traditional quality control often relies on manual inspection or rule-based systems that can be time-consuming and error-prone. Generative AI, on the other hand, can analyze data from multiple sensors, images, and production logs to identify anomalies and defects in real-time. By detecting issues early in the production process, AI-powered quality control systems help reduce waste, improve product quality, and lower costs. Companies like Siemens and Bosch are using AI-based image recognition systems to inspect products on the assembly line, detecting defects with a high degree of accuracy. This proactive approach to quality control enhances overall operational efficiency and ensures that products meet rigorous quality standards before they reach the market.

In addition to automation and quality control, generative AI enables businesses to harness predictive analytics for strategic decision-making. By analyzing historical data and generating future scenarios, AI models provide valuable insights that can guide decisions related to pricing, resource allocation, and risk management. For example, in the retail industry, generative AI can analyze customer behavior data to forecast demand for specific products, allowing companies to adjust pricing and promotional strategies accordingly. In finance, AI models can predict market trends and assess the risk of investment portfolios, enabling institutions to make more informed financial decisions. These predictive capabilities allow businesses to anticipate changes and make proactive adjustments, reducing the likelihood of costly mistakes and missed opportunities.

Generative AI is also transforming human resources by enabling data-driven hiring, training, and workforce management. AI-driven recruitment platforms can analyze resumes, social media profiles, and professional networks to identify candidates who are a strong match for open positions. This allows HR teams to streamline the recruitment process and focus on candidates who are most likely to succeed in the role. Beyond recruitment, generative AI can personalize employee training by creating tailored learning materials that address individual strengths and weaknesses. AI-powered learning platforms can assess employee performance, recommend specific courses or modules, and track progress over time. This personalized approach to training enhances employee skill development and boosts job satisfaction, ultimately benefiting the organization as a whole.

In workforce management, generative AI enables businesses to optimize staffing levels and improve scheduling accuracy. For instance, AI models can analyze historical attendance data, seasonal demand patterns, and employee preferences to create schedules that meet both business needs and employee expectations. In industries such as retail and healthcare, where staffing requirements can vary significantly, AI-powered scheduling tools help ensure that the right number of employees are available at all times, minimizing labor costs and improving service quality. Generative AI's ability to optimize workforce management enables businesses to operate more efficiently and create a positive work environment for employees.

Generative AI's impact on operational efficiency also extends to energy management. Companies in energy-intensive industries are using AI to monitor energy consumption and optimize usage patterns. By analyzing data from sensors and equipment, generative AI can identify inefficiencies, predict maintenance needs, and suggest adjustments to reduce energy waste. For example, in manufacturing,

AI models can monitor machinery performance in real-time, identifying signs of wear or potential malfunctions before they lead to costly downtime. Predictive maintenance not only extends the lifespan of equipment but also reduces operational disruptions, enabling companies to maintain a smooth production process. This approach to energy and asset management helps businesses reduce their environmental impact and achieve sustainability goals.

In addition, generative AI facilitates cybersecurity by detecting and responding to threats in real-time. Cybersecurity is a critical concern for modern businesses, and generative AI enables companies to monitor networks, analyze potential threats, and respond proactively to security incidents. AI models can analyze vast amounts of network traffic, identifying anomalies and flagging potential security breaches before they escalate. This proactive approach to cybersecurity helps companies protect sensitive data, maintain customer trust, and comply with regulatory requirements. By continuously analyzing security data and adapting to new threats, generative AI-based security solutions offer a level of protection that traditional systems cannot match, ensuring that businesses can operate with confidence in an increasingly complex digital landscape.

In conclusion, generative AI is driving a profound transformation in internal business operations. By automating routine tasks, optimizing supply chain management, enabling predictive analytics, and enhancing cybersecurity, AI empowers companies to operate more efficiently, make data-driven decisions, and respond to changing market conditions. As generative AI continues to evolve, businesses that embrace these advanced tools for internal operations will be better positioned to achieve sustainable growth and maintain a competitive edge in their respective industries.